# Foreword

*office*
## CHIEF RABBI

### FOREWORD BY THE CHIEF RABBI, DR JONATHAN SACKS

The publication of this long awaited book, which combines a dictionary of British Sign Language with an explanation of Jewish terms, is much to be welcomed. For far too long, the people of the Jewish Deaf community have not been able to access their religion in their own language – British Sign Language.

The introduction of the loop system into our synagogues enabled hearing aid users to participate in services. Now, sign language interpreted and explanatory synagogue services are providing sign language users with an opportunity to learn more about their culture and be a part of the synagogue life.

The initiatives of the Jewish Deaf Association are invaluable in ensuring that sign language users can rightfully feel a part of their Jewish heritage. As well as being an invaluable guide for interpreters and those studying Judaism in British Sign Language, this book provides a much needed addition to the growing provision for Deaf people within the Jewish community.

The preparation of this publication fills a long identified need. May the possession of this book be an enjoyment, an education and a blessing to those who use it.

*Jonathan Sacks*

Chief Rabbi, Dr Jonathan Sacks

לֹא עָלֶיךָ
הַמְּלָאכָה
לִגְמֹר
וְלֹא אַתָּה
בֶּן חוֹרִין
לְהִבָּטֵל
מִמֶּנָּה

Adler House 735 High Road London N12 0US Tel: 020 8343 6301 Fax: 020 8343 6310 info@chiefrabbi.org www.chiefrabbi.org

# Introduction

In 1996, whilst working as coordinator of Koleinu - a project supporting Jewish Deaf youth and children - Mira Goldberg was asked by a parent if she could recommend a book suitable for a Jewish Deaf youngster to learn about their religion and culture. On investigating, she was surprised to learn that no such thing existed - there were books in the USA and Israel, but none had been produced in British Sign Language.

Many elderly members of the Jewish Deaf Association had been educated at the Residential School for Jewish Deaf Children in London – the only Jewish school in the United Kingdom ever to be set up for the Deaf. It had opened in 1865 and, sadly, closed in 1965. Mira began to realise that many Jewish signs, which had evolved at this school, were in danger of being lost through generations. The preservation of the original signs of a unique community – the Anglo-Jewish Deaf Community - presented another reason to produce this book.

Little did Mira know how enormous and daunting the project would be and how long it would take to complete the book! From the outset, a committee was formed and its members Eva Fielding-Jackson, Irene Spielsinger and Issy Schlisselman worked with Mira throughout the project.

This book is aimed at parents of deaf children, rabbis, British Sign Language tutors, interpreters and anyone else with an interest in BSL and basic Judaism. All the signs shown in the book are for right-handed signers. Left-handed signers should reverse the signs.

It is assumed that the readers will already know basic British Sign Language, hence any signs which are part of our general vocabulary are not shown. Only the signs that are unique to Judaism are included in the book.

If there is a word related to Judaism which is not featured in the book, it does not mean that the word is not significant – simply that there is no recognised BSL sign for it (e.g. Talmud).

In order to be as user-friendly as possible, the book focuses on traditional Anglo-Jewish practice and does not go into the various traditions in other countries.

# Acknowledgements

*left to right:*
*Issy Schlisselman,*
*Eva Fielding-Jackson,*
*Mira Goldberg,*
*Irene Spielsinger*

Heartfelt thanks to everyone who helped with the creation of this book:

The Duveen Trust, The Kessler Foundation (which is funded by the Jewish Chronicle), Reading Hebrew Congregation and Tzivos Hashem, who recognised its worth and so generously contributed towards the costs; Norwood Child Care and Ravenswood (as they were then) for their initial support; John Adler for his advice and guidance; Alan Greenbat OBE JP at the Office of The Chief Rabbi whose patience and support has been very deeply appreciated; Sharon Graham whose expertise in PR and marketing has been invaluable; David Jackson who spent many hours ensuring the high quality of the photography and the members of the JDA who sat through lengthy photo sessions; Martin Bogard for additional help with photography; the proof readers and those who took the time and trouble to give their feedback on the arrows relating to the signs; the Jewish Deaf Association who embraced this project, supported the committee and for whose encouragement and backing I will always be grateful; and everyone who may not be named who gave their help and cooperation towards producing this long-awaited publication.

Last, but not least, my very special thanks go to the committee - Eva Fielding-Jackson, Issy Schlisselman and Irene Spielsinger – without whose dedication, hard work and commitment this book would never have materialised.

Thank you all.


Mira Goldberg
Book Project Leader

# How to use the book

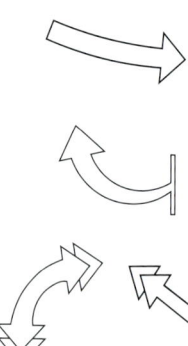

1) A single smooth stroke in direction of the pictured arrow

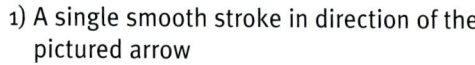

2) One hand pauses. Other hand moves in direction of the pictured arrow

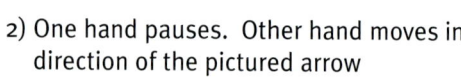

3) A single smooth stroke backwards and forwards in direction of arrow

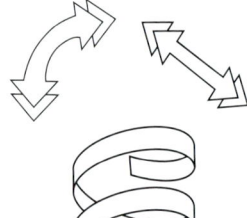

4) A single smooth stroke in a rolling tunnel in direction of the pictured arrow

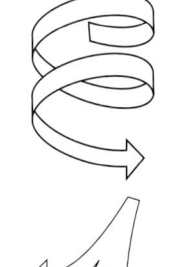

5) Start with clenched fists, then spread outwards

6) A circular stroke against the palm, repeatedly in direction of the arrow

7) Two hands criss-cross in direction of the pictured arrow

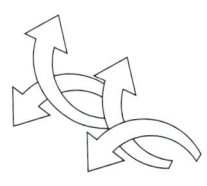

= Sign

= Pronunciation

Accentuate syllable in **bold**

# Contents

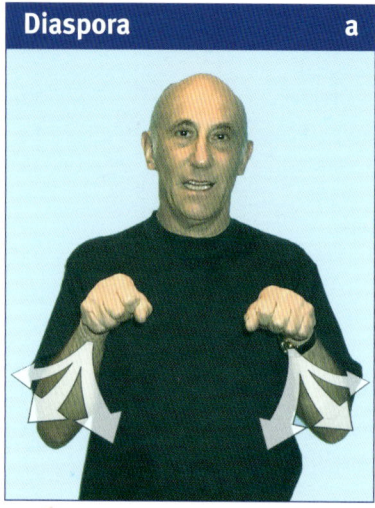

**Diaspora**       a

 **Clenched fists open downwards**

 Dai-**ass**-pra

The word Diaspora (Galut) refers to Jewish communities based in countries other than Israel.  It is derived from the word 'dispersion', which describes how the Jewish people have been scattered to countries around the world, as a result of persecution, war and exile.

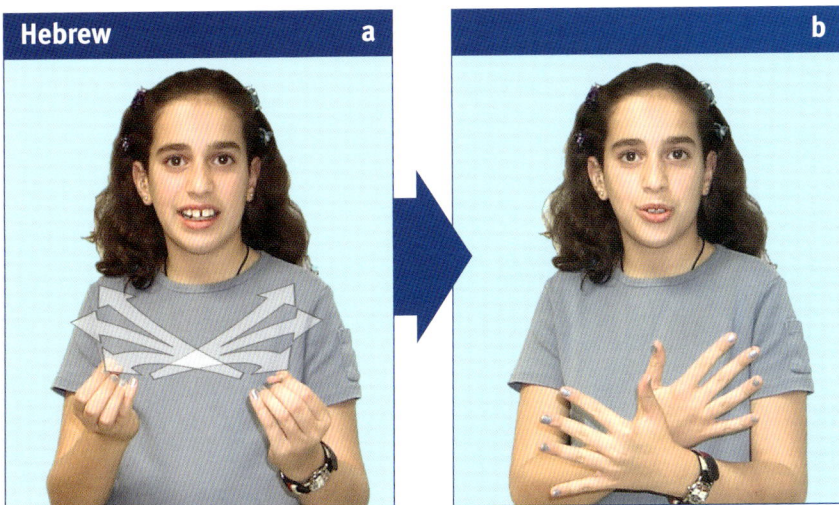

**Hebrew** a

b

 **Fingertips together cross over and open**

Hebrew is the ancient language of the Jews. In the past century, it has evolved to the more modern format used in Israel today, which is known as Ivrit.

Words are written from right to left and all books read from right to left.

The Hebrew alphabet consists of twenty-two consonants. Five of these take a special form at the end of words, and are then called 'final letters'. The 'finals' are pronounced in the same way as their corresponding letters in the main alphabet, but are written differently.

With the alphabet, there is a system of vowels which are written above, below or next to the appropriate letter.

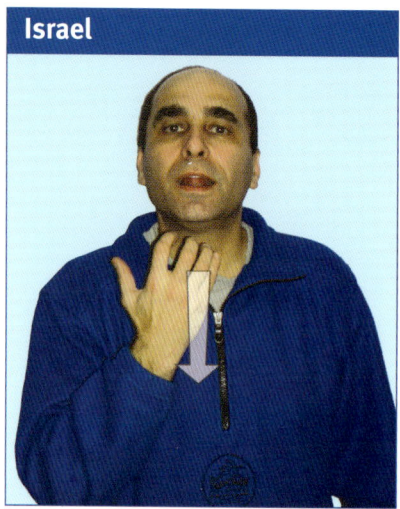

Israel

 **Sign from chin outwards**

On the 5th of Iyar 5708 (15th May 1948), the State of Israel was established. Previously the Jews had not had a homeland of their own for two thousand years and were dispersed across the world (the Diaspora).

After the Second World War, the United Nations voted for the present State of Israel to be established.

Israel Independence Day is celebrated throughout the Jewish world.  In Israel it is a public holiday.

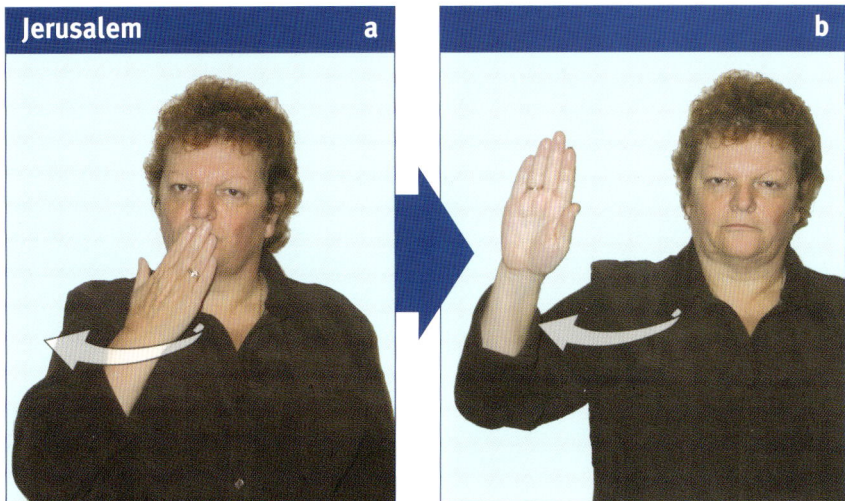

Jerusalem    a       b

Until 1967, Jerusalem was a divided city, in which only the New City belonged to Israel. The Old City, which contains sites holy to all three major religions, was under Jordanian control. In the 1967 Six-Day War, Israel gained control of the entire city and since that time it has remained united as the capital of Israel.

# Judaism in General

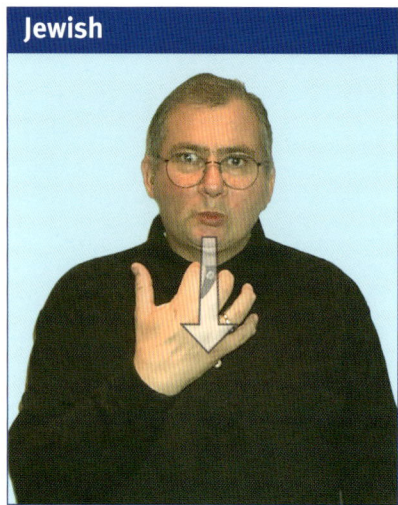

**Jewish**

 **Sign from chin outwards**

According to Jewish law, anyone who is born of a Jewish mother is regarded as Jewish.

A non-Jew can convert to Judaism by taking a course and examination set by the religious authorities.

# Judaism in General

**Orthodox** (1st version)

**Orthodox** (2nd version)

Sign like 'beating your chest' twice

Index fingers spiral from ears downwards twice

**Orthodox** (3rd version)    a    b

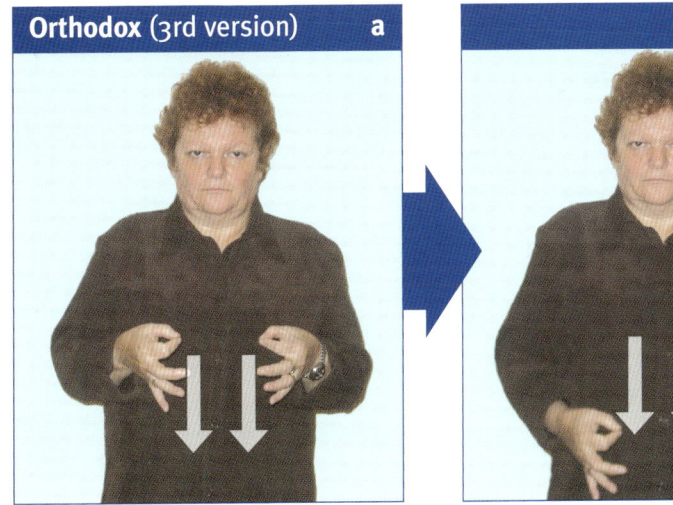

Someone who is observant of all Jewish laws and customs is described as Orthodox.

**Frum** a

 **Use pouted lips. Crooked index finger tap on palm twice**

 Froom ("oo"=not oo as in "room" but oo as in "book")

The word 'Frum' is used to describe someone who strictly observes all the laws and customs of Judaism.

This is an everyday Yiddish word referring to traditional Jewish practice. It originates from the German word 'fromm', meaning religious.

# Judaism in General

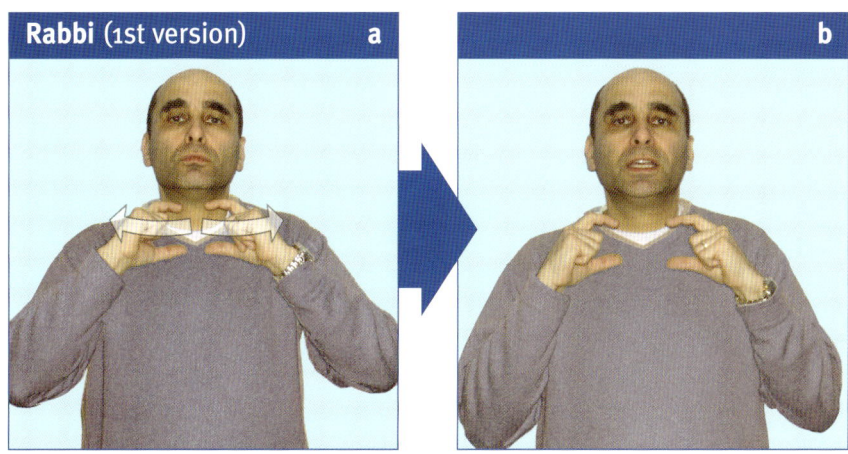

**Rabbi** (1st version)   a | b

🖐 **'C' hand shape across neck twice**

👄 *Rab*-i ("i"=like "eye")

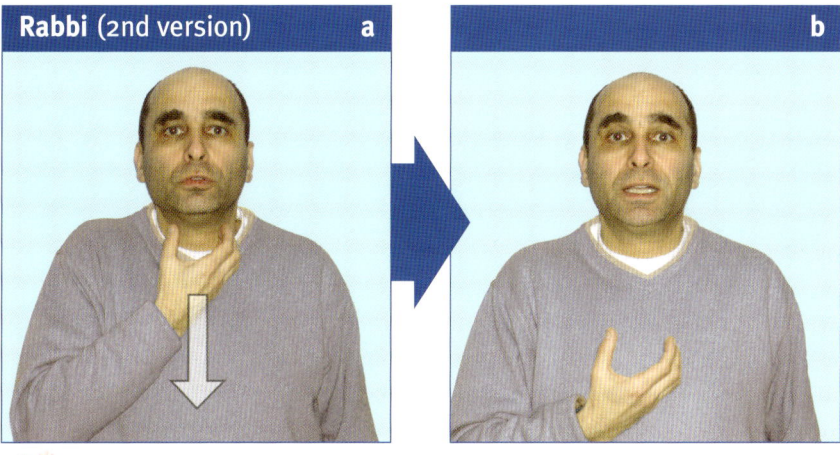

**Rabbi** (2nd version)   a | b

🖐 **Sign like 'Beard'**

👄 *Rab*-i ("i"=like "eye")

Rabbi is a Hebrew word meaning 'my teacher' and is a Jewish religious leader who has obtained a recognised qualification in Jewish knowledge. This act of qualification is called "Semicha".

A rabbi is a qualification, not a profession, except in the case of a teacher or the leader of a congregation.

# Judaism in General

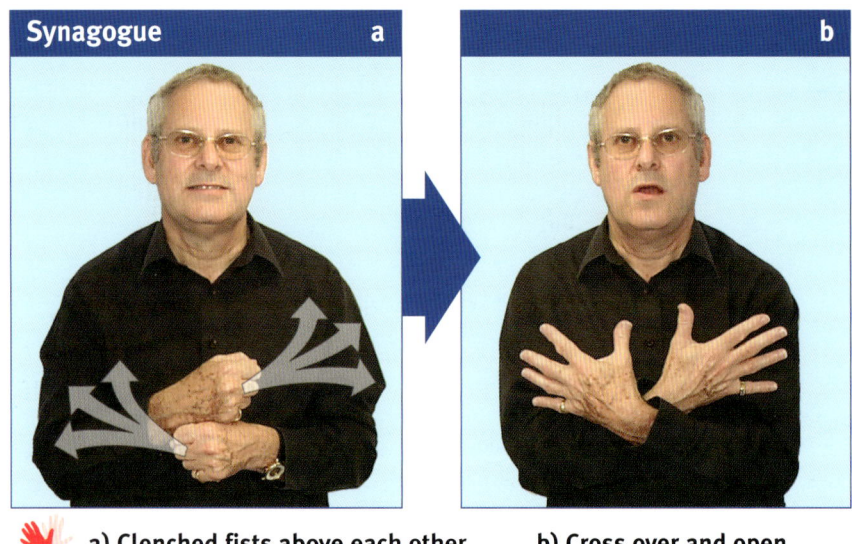

| Synagogue | a | | b |
|---|---|---|---|

a) Clenched fists above each other      b) Cross over and open

**Sin**-a-gog ("sin" as in doing something wrong)

A synagogue is a house of meeting for Jewish people.  It is often called a Shul (pronounced Shool).  The synagogue forms the heart of Jewish social, educational, cultural and religious life, hosting services, activities, religion classes and day centres.

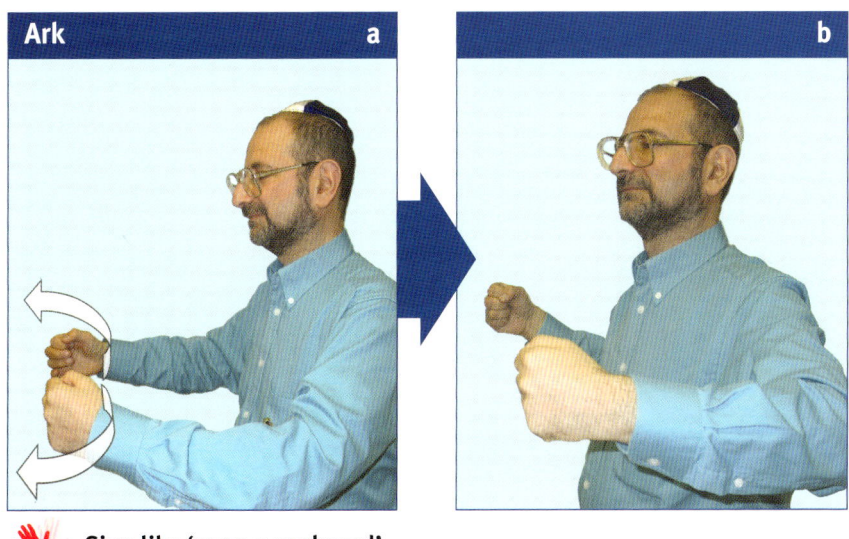

**Ark** a | b

🖐 **Sign like 'open a cupboard'**

Each synagogue keeps its bible scrolls in a cupboard called the Ark.
This forms a central part of the synagogue. Wherever possible, it is situated at the wall nearest to Jerusalem. The Ark itself is protective of the scrolls and has both a door and a curtain.

The scrolls are very expensive to produce as they are written by hand and are often donated to the synagogue. They are treated with great care and the Ark keeps them safe until needed.

When the Ark is opened to take out or replace the scrolls during a service, the congregation stands as a mark of respect.

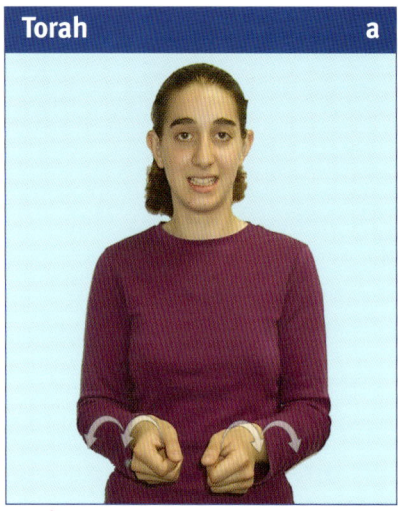

**Torah**　　　　　　　　　　　a

 **Twist hands twice outwards**

 *Tor*-ah

The Torah is the Five Books of Moses and the oral law derived from them.

The Torah is carefully handwritten on parchment scrolls by skilled men. The scrolls are very precious and, because they are so expensive to produce, are often donated to the synagogue. A scroll - 'Sefer Torah' – is most precious and kept in the Ark.

Every Shabbat (Sabbath) at the synagogue consecutive chapters are read from the scrolls.

# Jewish Customs and Traditions

## Kiddush

 **Sign like 'drinking from a cup'**

 *Kid*-ish

The ceremony of Kiddush represents the blessing of the wine and another blessing of the challah (bread) at Sabbath and Festivals. It is carried out both in the synagogue and at home.

A Kiddush cup is filled with wine (a traditional symbol of joy) and a blessing is said in Hebrew, which means:

*Bless you Lord, our God, King of the universe, who creates the fruit of the vine.*

Everyone at the table drinks. After this, the hands are washed and a short blessing is said. The challah (bread) is blessed and cut, then dipped in a little salt - except at New Year (Rosh Hashanah), when honey is used. A piece is given to each person at the table. From the moment of washing the hands until the eating of the bread, apart from the blessings, no words are spoken.

# Jewish Customs and Traditions

**Challah**       a        b

Sign like 'plaiting dough'

*Ha*-la

In order that bread should be kosher, it is important that a symbolic portion of the dough is removed and not used. The removed portion is called 'challah'. This practice dates back to biblical times, when a tenth of a person's income was given to the priest (Cohen) and the Levites who, by working full-time in the Temple, were unable to support themselves and their families.

Challah loaves (plaited or round) are used in the Kiddush ceremony on Sabbath (Shabbat) and Holy Days (Yom Tov).

# Jewish Customs and Traditions

## Kippah (skullcap)

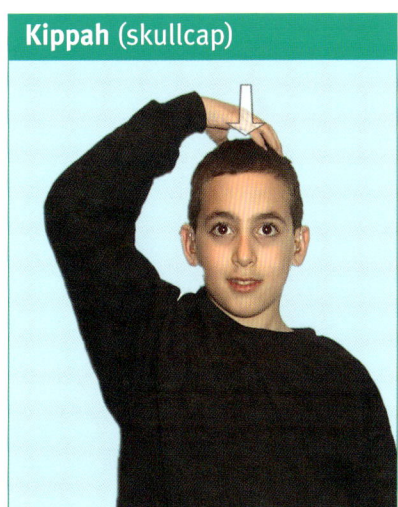

 Ki-**pah** ('ki' as in kip)

A kippah is the round head-covering (or skullcap) worn by orthodox Jewish men, as a sign of their respect for God.

Variations on the word include: yarmulkah, kapel or cupple.

# Jewish Customs and Traditions

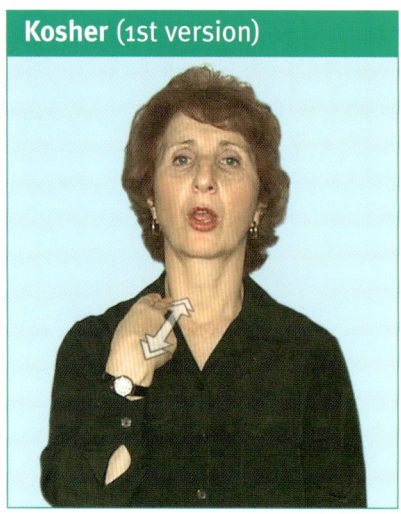

**Kosher** (1st version)

 **Two fingers tap the neck**

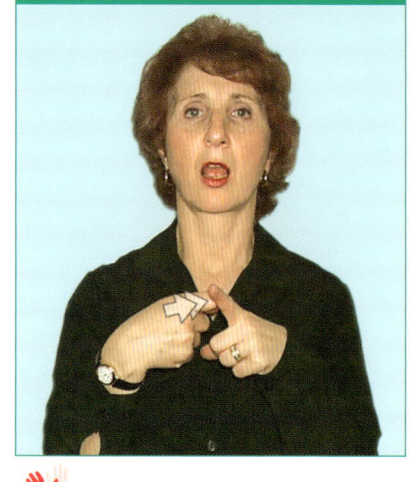

**Kosher** (2nd version)

 **'K' letter**

The word 'kosher' means 'suitable'. The distinction between what is kosher and what is not is explained in Jewish law. Food, clothing, cutlery, crockery, saucepans and all religious items are specially prepared so that they are kosher.

Instructions not to mix meat with milk come from a command in the Five Books of Moses (Torah). In traditional practice, there is a clear break between the eating of meat and the eating of dairy produce. Separate sets of kitchenware, crockery and cutlery are used for meat and dairy meals.

Jewish people may only eat from animals that chew the cud and also have cloven (divided) hooves. For meat, animals must be slaughtered as quickly and painlessly as possible. To ensure this, the slaughtering must only be undertaken by a Shochet – a specially trained, religiously observant man. After slaughter, meat needs to be washed carefully, salted and left to stand so that the salt absorbs the blood, which can then be washed away. In Jewish tradition, blood represents life and must not be eaten because this would be like eating an animal that is still alive.

Various types of fowl are permitted - such as chickens, ducks, geese and turkeys. However, many birds are forbidden, including all birds of prey.

Only fish with fins and scales are allowed, so shellfish, prawns and creatures such as eels are not kosher.

# Jewish Customs and Traditions

## Mezzuzah

 **Index finger and thumb down palm**

 Mez-*oo*-za ("oo"=not oo as in "room" but oo as in "book")

A mezzuzah is a small scroll in a protective covering.  The text of the scroll contains biblical verses.  In traditional practice, a mezzuzah is fixed to the doorpost of every room in the Jewish house, including the front and back entrances but excluding bathrooms and toilets.

The casing is often decorated and may be made of wood, metal, plastic, enamel, glass or even china.

There is a tradition for people to kiss the mezzuzah when entering or leaving the house.  Awareness of the mezzuzah is a reminder of the presence of God.

# Jewish Customs and Traditions

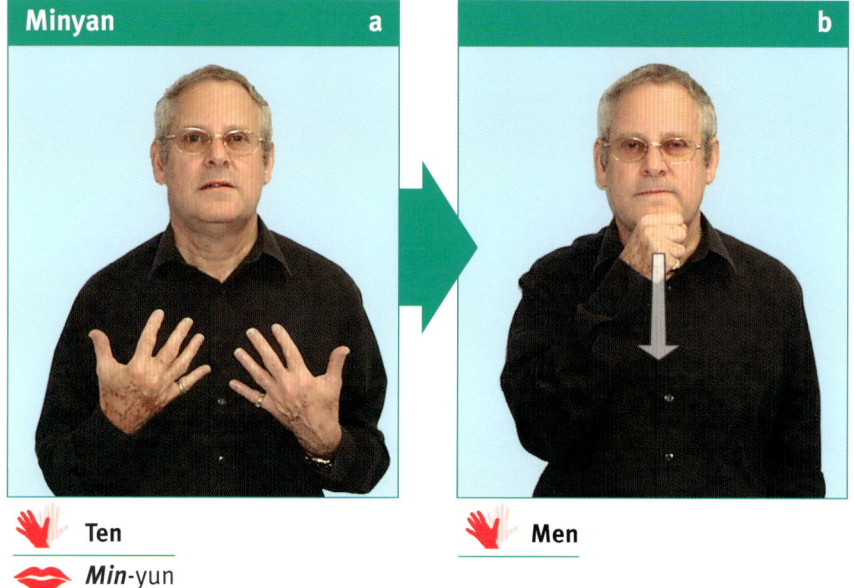

**Minyan**   a     b

**Ten**
*Min*-yun

**Men**

A Minyan consists of ten men over the age of thirteen years. This is the minimum requirement for public worship.

# Jewish Customs and Traditions

**Peyot**

 **Index fingers spiral from ears downwards twice**

 Pe-*yot* ("e"=like "pet")

Peyot are the 'ringlets' of hair (looking like long sideburns) that are grown by certain groups of men, carrying out the instruction in the Five Books of Moses (Torah) that the temples must never be shaved.

Awareness of the peyot is a reminder of the presence of God.

# Jewish Customs and Traditions

**Talit**

 Ta-*lit*

A Talit is a fringed prayer shawl worn by men at prayer in the synagogue.

# Jewish Customs and Traditions

**Tefillin**       a

 **Wind clenched fist around still arm towards wrist**

 Te-*fill*-in

The Five Books of Moses (Torah) give the instruction to "bind the words of Torah on your hands and between your eyes". This is put into practice by the use of Tefillin - two small black leather boxes containing scrolls with Biblical quotations written on them. Used only by men who have reached the age of Barmitzvah, the Tefillin boxes have straps attached to them which are wound round the head and arm whilst morning prayers are being recited on weekdays.

*Reproduced with kind permission ©David Rose*

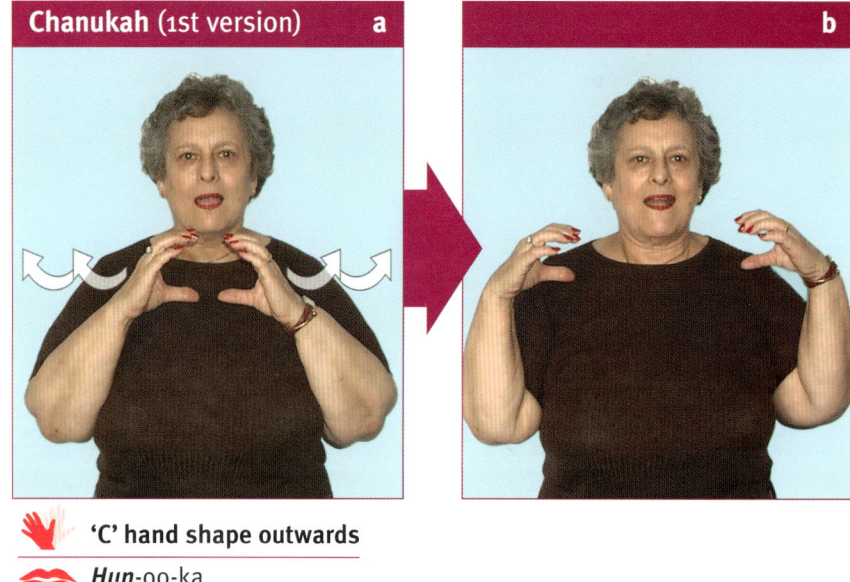

**Chanukah** (1st version)  a  b

**'C' hand shape outwards**

*Hun*-oo-ka

Chanukah is a joyous festival that falls in mid-winter. The name Chanukah comes from the Hebrew word 'Dedication' and is the celebration of the re-dedication of the Temple.

The story of Chanukah is about the bravery of Judah the Maccabee and his battle against the Syrians in the 2nd century before the Common Era. The Syrians had persecuted the Jews and desecrated their holy Temple. Judah and his family fought them and repossessed the Temple, but it was badly damaged and, most importantly, the eternal flame inside no longer burned.

They found a small jar of 'consecrated' oil (prepared in a special way) – but only enough to keep the eternal flame burning for one day. They needed at least eight days to consecrate a new supply. They lit the lamp, expecting the oil to run out by the next day – but, instead, the jar became full again and was miraculously refilled each night, giving eight days of light and enough time to prepare a new supply of consecrated oil.

*continue next page*

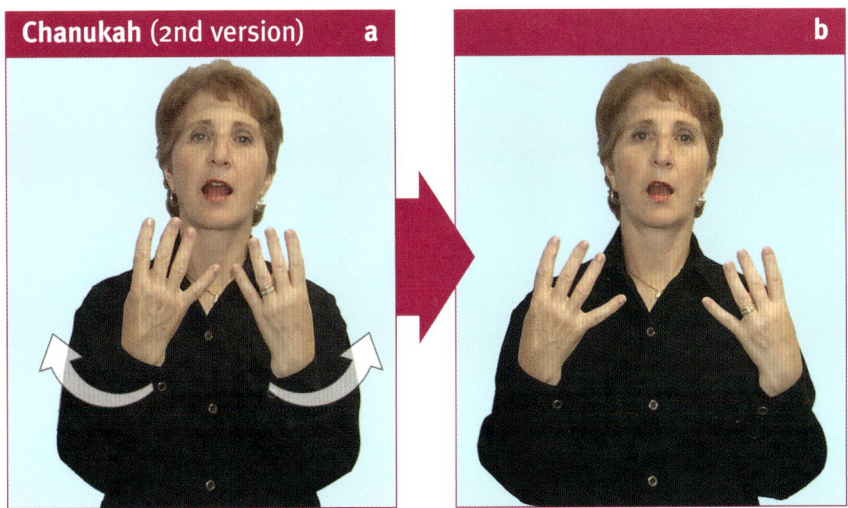

**Chanukah** (2nd version)   a     b

It is traditional to light Chanukah candles for eight days.  Each candle represents one day of the miracle.

The candles are displayed on a nine-branched candle holder called a Chanukiya or Menorah.  Eight of the candles are placed at the same level but there is one candle which is separate.  This is called the Shamash, which means 'caretaker'.  The Shamash is lit first, representing the miracle jar.  It is then used to light the other candles.  One extra candle is lit each day until, on the eighth day, all the candles are lit together.

## Dreidel

 **Sign like 'spinning top'**

 *Drey*-dl

A dreidel is a small spinning top with four sides, used to play a game of chance at Chanukah.  In Hebrew, it is called a Sevivon.

On each side of the dreidel there are Hebrew letters that represent the words 'Nes Gadol Haya Sham', which mean 'A Big Miracle Happened There'.  The words remind players of the story of Chanukah.

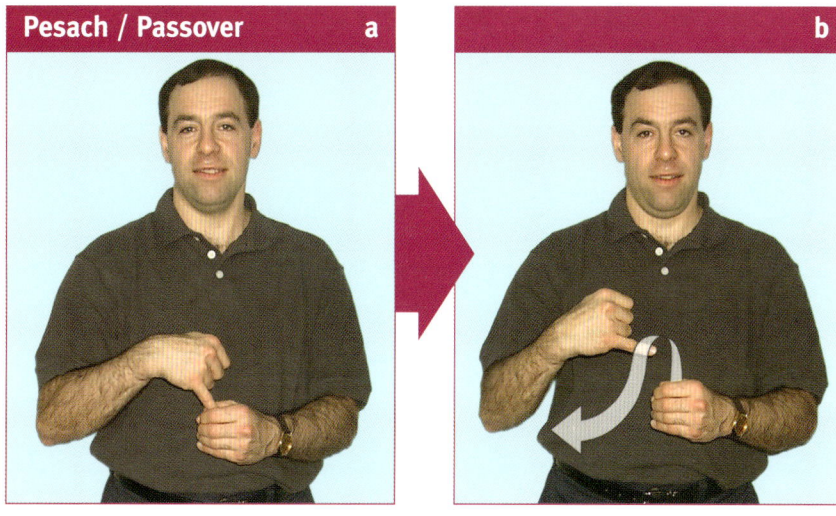

**Pesach / Passover**    a       b

*Pe*-sah ("pe" as in "pet") / ***Pass***-over

Pesach (Passover) – the festival of Spring - lasts eight days and commemorates the story of how the Children of Israel were rescued from slavery in Egypt and led to freedom.

A special gathering, known as a Seder, is held in Jewish homes and communities on the first and second evenings of Passover.  This is to enable Jewish people to celebrate their freedom and remind themselves and their families of the miracles God performed to enable them to leave the land of their slavery.

Only specially supervised food is permitted during the festival of Passover and, before the festival, a thorough cleansing of all rooms and cupboards is undertaken, to remove every trace of non-permitted foods.

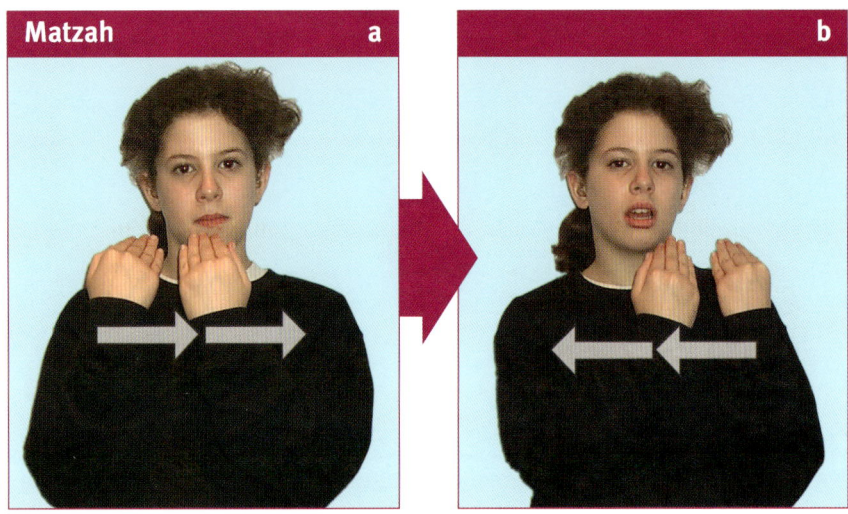

**Matzah**  a  b

Another version – sign on one hand only

*Mut*-za ("mut" as in "cut")

During the festival of Passover (Pesach), it is forbidden to eat leavened (risen) food.  This is to commemorate the speedy escape from slavery in Egypt, when there was no time for the bread to rise.

Instead of bread, unleavened bread is eaten during this time.  This is called Matzah.

Similar to a water biscuit, matzah can be ground into a fine powder and used in cooking/baking instead of breadcrumbs.

Matzah can be eaten all year round but anything eaten at Passover (Pesach) must be produced under strictly controlled conditions to be approved as 'Kosher for Pesach'.

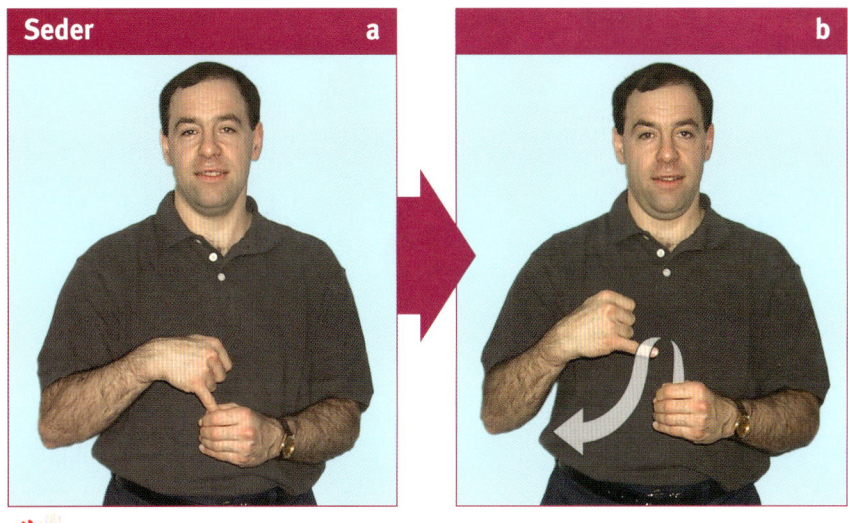

**Seder** a b

W | **Repeat twice**

👄 | **Sey**-der

The Seder is the special family evening service and meal which takes place on the first and second nights of Passover (Pesach) to celebrate the freedom of the Jewish people from slavery in Egypt.

A book called the Haggadah is used to tell of the slavery, the exodus and the parting of the Red Sea.

The table is laid with special care; everyone has a wine goblet and in the centre of the table is an extra glass of wine for the prophet Elijah, whose presence is strongly felt during the Seder service.

Food eaten at the Seder meal is full of symbolism. Bread eaten must be unleavened (matzah), to remind Jews that, when escaping from slavery in Egypt, they had no time to allow their dough to rise before they left on their journey to the Promised Land.

Various symbolic foods and herbs are displayed on a Seder plate and referred to during the service. Some of these items will be eaten, including a bitter vegetable such as horseradish, to represent the bitter lives of the Jews while they were slaves.

The first course of the Seder meal is a hard-boiled egg, in salt water. The egg represents life, birth, death and renewal and the unending story of the Jewish people. The salt water represents the tears shed by the Children of Israel as they endured their slavery.

**Purim**        **a**        **b**

**'B' hands open downwards**

***Poor*-im**

On the 14th day of Adar (around March), Purim is celebrated. The name Purim is derived from the word 'pur' meaning lot or lottery.

The story of Purim tells how a beautiful Jewish girl, Esther, and her uncle Mordechai saved the Jews living in Persia from almost certain destruction by proving their loyalty to the King, Ahasuerus. The King's chief minister, Haman, tried to turn the King against the Jews. He organised a lottery to choose a suitable date on which to destroy the Jews and the 14th of Adar was picked. However, his plan was ruined.

In the synagogue, the book of Esther, containing the story of Purim, is read. When Haman's name is mentioned, it is traditional to make loud noises with rattles (Ra'ashans) or by stamping feet.

At Purim, it is traditional to hold fancy dress parties and wear masks.

It is also customary to give food parcels (anonymously) to the poor and to eat small cakes called Hamantashen.

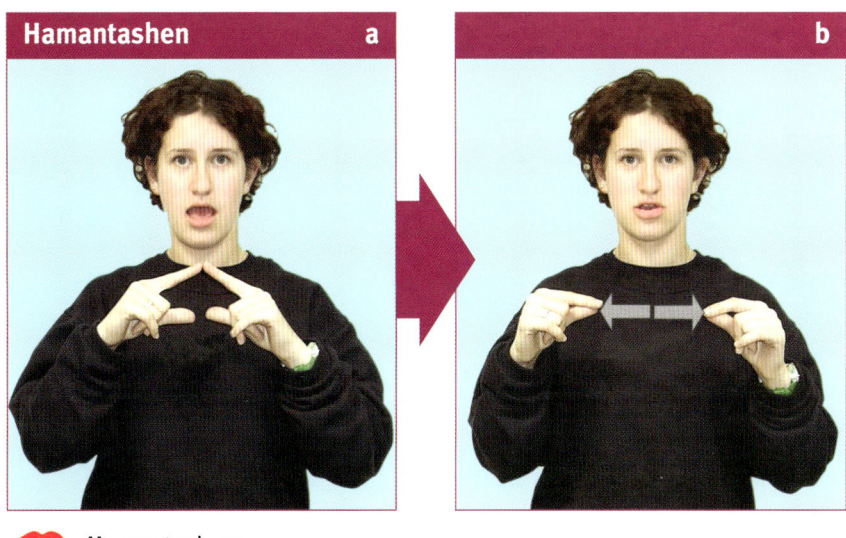

**Hamantashen** a / b

*Ha*-mn-tash-en

Hamantashen are small, triangular, sweet cakes, usually filled with poppy seeds. They are traditionally eaten during Purim. Named after Haman, one of the principal characters in the Purim story, some say the name derives from the words 'Ozen Haman' (Haman's ears) and others say it comes from 'Taschen Haman' (Haman's pockets).

# Jewish Calendar - Rosh Hashanah

**Rosh Hashanah** (New Year)    **a**                                      **b**

**New**                                       **Year**

Rosh Ha-*sha*-na ("osh"=like "gosh")

Rosh Hashanah is one of the names for the New Year in Hebrew. This is the term that most people use. Rosh means 'head' and Hashanah means 'the year'.

Rosh Hashanah falls in the month of Tishri (September/October). It is observed for two days, both in Israel and in the Diaspora.

Rosh Hashanah is a time for prayer and repentance, rather than celebration. During the ten days between Rosh Hashanah and Yom Kippur (Day of Atonement), Jewish people repent for their sins and ask God for forgiveness.

It is also traditional to give money to charity (Tzedakah), so that sins may be forgiven.

At the Kiddush service on Rosh Hashanah, it is traditional to eat apple and honey as the symbol of a sweet new year. When eating the challah (bread), it is the custom to use honey instead of salt.

**Shofar**

 **Show**-fa

The shofar is a ram's horn that is blown during New Year (Rosh Hashanah), calling on people to repent their sins. It is symbolic of the ram's horn caught in the thicket (bush) during the binding of Isaac. This forms the Biblical reading of the second day of the festival.

The shofar is also blown daily throughout the month of Ellul, before Rosh Hashanah. It is not blown on Shabbat.

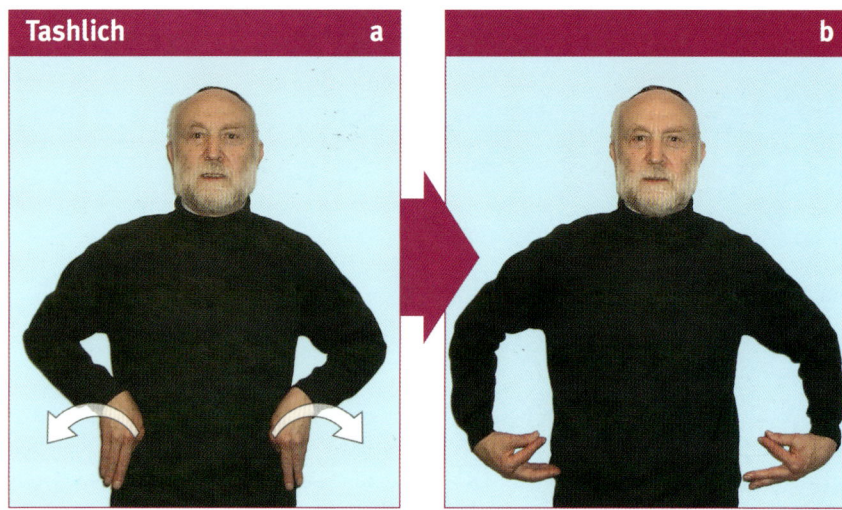

| Tashlich a | b |

 **Sign like 'pull out your pockets'**

*Tash*-lik

Tashlich is a ceremony performed at New Year (Rosh Hashanah) symbolising the casting away of one's sins. It consists of going to an area of flowing water. In some communities, people empty their pockets into the moving water to symbolise the hope that their sins will be washed away.

## Shabbat / Sabbath

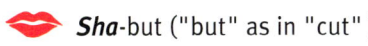 **Sha**-but ("but" as in "cut" )

Shabbat (Sabbath) is a day of rest, starting on Friday evening about half an hour before sunset and ending on Saturday at nightfall. Apart from the Day of Atonement (Yom Kippur), Shabbat is regarded as the most important time in the Jewish calendar. The observance of Shabbat takes priority over everything except the saving of life. Work is forbidden on Shabbat, including any act that can be interpreted as work.

On Friday night, just before Shabbat starts, candles are lit. Married women wear a head cover for the ceremony. Whilst lighting the candles they say a prayer in Hebrew which means:

*Bless you Lord, our God, King of the universe who sanctified us with his commandments and commanded us to light the Sabbath candles.*

**Shavuot**

 **Shake 'good' hand shapes together**

 Sha-voo-*ot*

The wheat harvest is celebrated at Shavuot, which comes seven weeks after Pesach. Also known as the Feast of Weeks, the Festival of Harvest and Pentecost, it is the festival that celebrates the giving of the Ten Commandments.

During Shavuot it is traditional to eat dairy food, especially cheesecake and blintzes.

During the festival, the Book of Ruth is read, as her story is directly related to the wheat harvest.

**Simchat** a

**Torah** b

🖐 **Happy**

👄 *Sim*-hut *Tor*-rah

🖐 **Twist hands twice outwards**

This festival is known as the 'Rejoicing of the Law'. It follows Succot and is one of the most joyous festivals in the Jewish calendar.

Each Saturday (Shabbat) in synagogue, a consecutive portion of the bible scroll (Torah) is read. It takes a year to complete the reading of the Torah. Simchat Torah is the time in the Jewish year when the Torah has been read from beginning to end.

The last chapters of the old cycle and the first chapter of the new cycle are read. All the scrolls are removed from the Ark and carried with joy, while the congregation dances with them around the raised platform in the centre of the synagogue (Bimah).

Women throw sweets and nuts and it is a time of great celebration.

**Succot**

 **Shake 'good' hand shapes together**

 Soo-*cot* ("oo"=not oo as in "room"but oo as in "book")

Five days after the Day of Atonement (Yom Kippur), Succot is celebrated. This is The Feast of Tabernacles. Succot commemorates the 40 years that the Children of Israel spent in the desert, after escaping from slavery in Egypt.

As Succot is associated with agriculture, Jewish people make a blessing over four different species of plants and fruit. The 'Four Species' of Plant/Fruit used at Succot during prayers are:

1. 'Lulav' - palm leaf branch

2. 'Arava' - a branch from a willow tree

3. 'Haddas' - a branch from the myrtle bush. The Haddas is associated with peace, since the dove was holding a myrtle twig in its mouth when it returned to Noah's Ark.

4. 'Etrog' – a citrus fruit.

The Lulav, Arava and Haddas are bound together and held next to the Etrog. A blessing is made over them and they are waved in all directions – forwards, backwards, sideways, upwards and downwards.

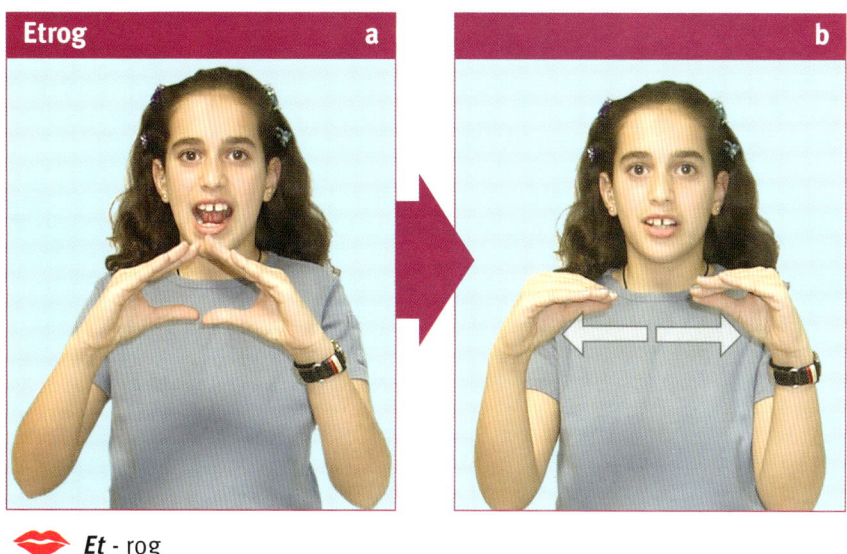

**Etrog** a     b

*Et* - rog

An Etrog is a citrus fruit that looks like a lemon and has a strong smell and flavour.  It is one of the 'Four Species' blessed at Succot (The Feast of Tabernacles).

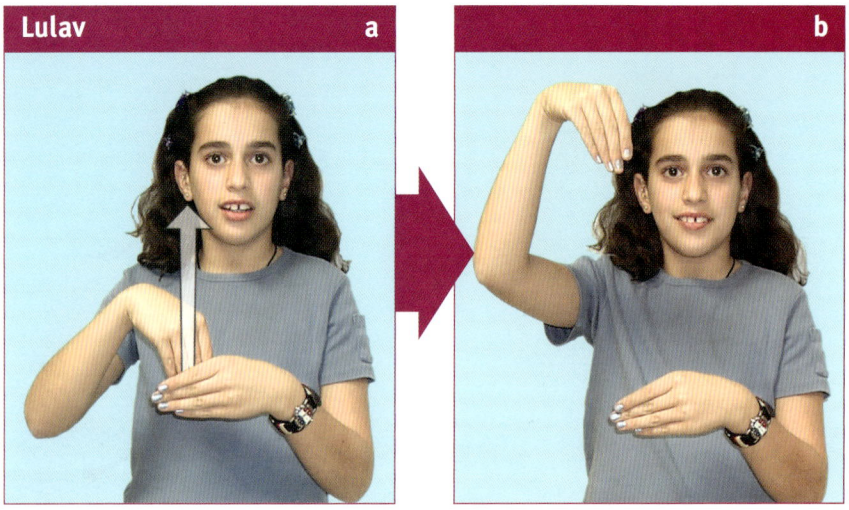

**Loo**-lav ("oo"=not oo as in "room" but oo as in "book")

A Lulav is a palm branch that has no smell or taste. It is one of the 'Four Species' blessed at Succot (The Feast of Tabernacles).

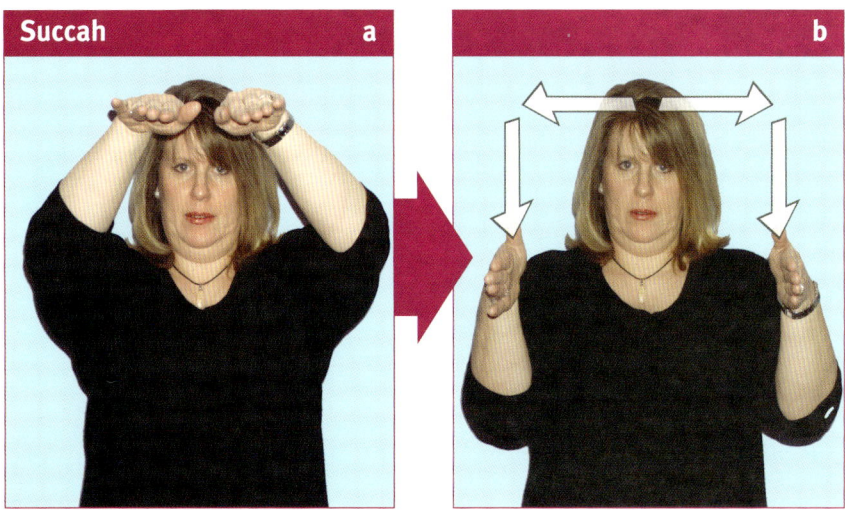

**Succah** a    b

💋 **Soo**-ca ("oo"=not oo as in "room"but oo as in "book")

During the years that the Children of Israel spent in the desert, they mostly ate, drank, lived and slept in the open air, with only leaves, twigs and tents for protection. To remind themselves of this, Jewish people erect a hut, called a Succah, next to their homes. They eat all their meals here for seven days, weather permitting. If the climate allows, they often sleep in the Succah too.

The roof of the Succah is made of branches, to enable people to see the sky. Fruits and vegetables are hung from the roof and the Succah is usually decorated to make it more beautiful.

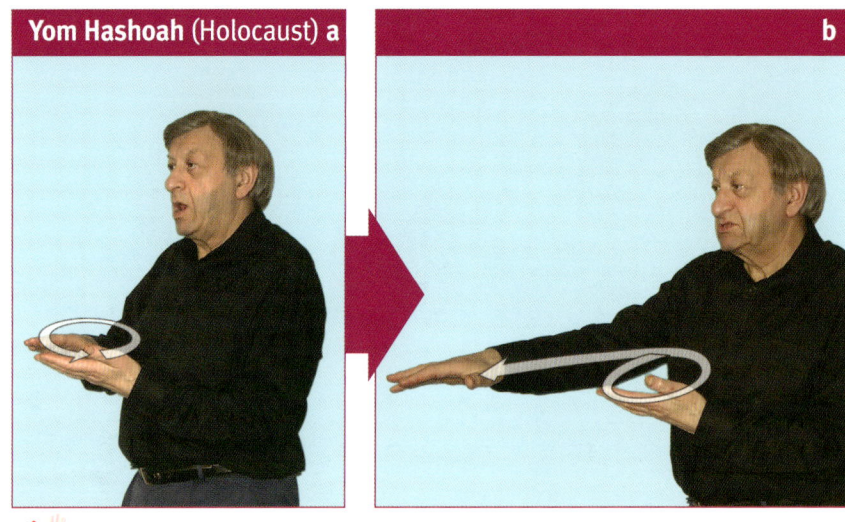

**Yom Hashoah** (Holocaust) **a**  **b**

**Wipe anti-clockwise**

Yom Ha-***show***-a

It is important to remember the Holocaust and it is considered that Jewish people have a duty to tell others about it, in an effort to ensure that such things are never repeated.

On Yom Hashoah, which falls on the 27th day of Nissan (around April/May), a day of mourning is observed, to commemorate the six million Jewish people who died during the Second World War.

Some people light memorial (Yahrzeit) candles on Yom Hashoah in memory of their loved ones who died in the Holocaust.

British Holocaust Memorial Day falls on 27th January each year.

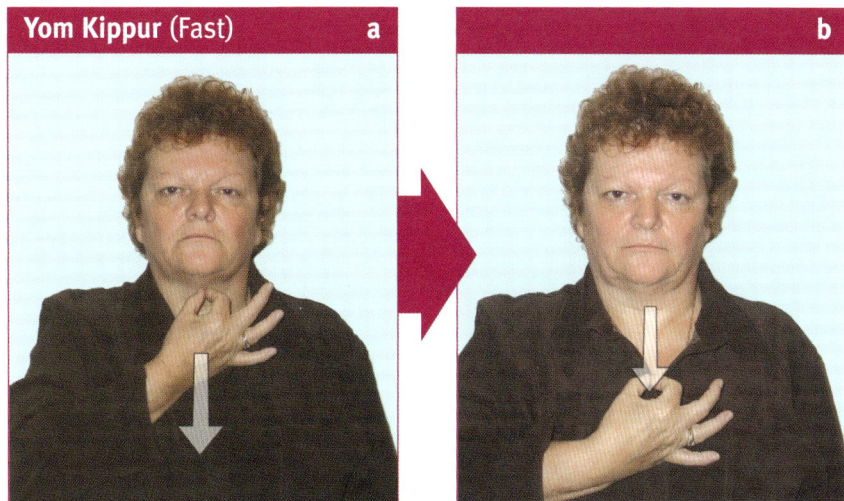

**Yom Kippur** (Fast)  a    b

 **'perfect' hand shape outwards from neck**

 Yom Kip-*oor* ("kip"=like "rip")

Yom Kippur (the Day of Atonement) is the holiest day of the Jewish Year. It is regarded as the 'Sabbath of Sabbaths'. This is the day on which Jewish people ask God to forgive them for all their sins.

It is believed that on this day God judges each person's actions, and each person's future is decided for the coming year.

From the eve of Yom Kippur (known as Kol Nidre), Jewish people fast for a total of twenty-five hours. No healthy person should consume food or drink throughout this period. There should be no work, no idle pleasure - just true repentance.

There is an evening synagogue service on Kol Nidre and an all day service on Yom Kippur, finishing when the fast ends with the sounding of the Shofar (ram's horn) at nightfall.

# Jewish Cycle of Life - Childhood

**Bar Mitzvah** / Bat Mitzvah

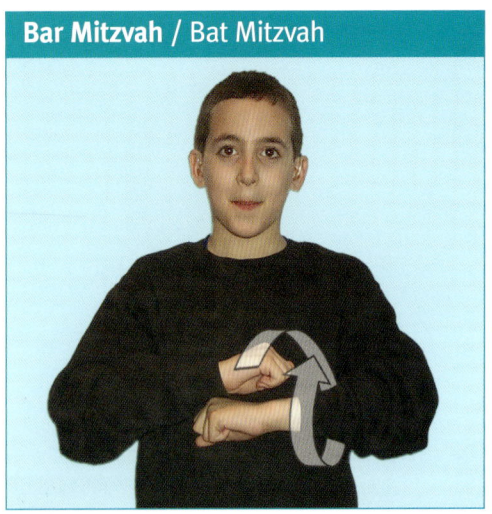

 **Wind both fists clockwise around each other**

 (Bar Mitzvah) Bar- *Mitz*-va / (Bat Mitzvah) Bat-*Mitz*-va

A boy becomes Bar Mitzvah when he is thirteen. A girl becomes Bat Mitzvah when she is twelve. They prepare for many months before their Bar/Bat Mitzvah, by learning the part of the bible scroll (Torah) that will be read in the synagogue on the day of their ceremony.

The term Bat Chayil is often used in place of Bat Mitzvah. The words Bat Chayil also refer to the preparation of a girl to become a woman.

A Mitzvah is a command to do one's duty. Bar Mitzvah, Bat Mitzvah or Bat Chayil means that a child is now personally responsible for fulfilling the requirements of Judaism and all its commands. They have come of age and are responsible for their actions. The Bar and Bat Mitzvah ceremony marks the point after which a person is required to observe the commandments and is therefore seen as the beginning of a new phase of a young person's life. This is a proud occasion, greatly celebrated.

# Jewish Cycle of Life - Childhood

## Brit Milah (circumcision)

 Brit-*Mi*-lah

In the Bible, God tells Abraham to make sure that every newborn boy is circumcised on the 8th day after his birth, by having the foreskin removed from his penis. If the baby is ill or not strong enough, the ceremony has to be postponed until he recovers. A Mohel - a specially trained man - carries out the circumcision. The Brit Milah is a sign of the covenant between God and the Jewish people and means the child can now be officially named. The Brit Milah ceremony is followed by a celebration.

# Jewish Cycle of Life - Childhood

**Cheder** (Hebrew School)    a

Hebrew

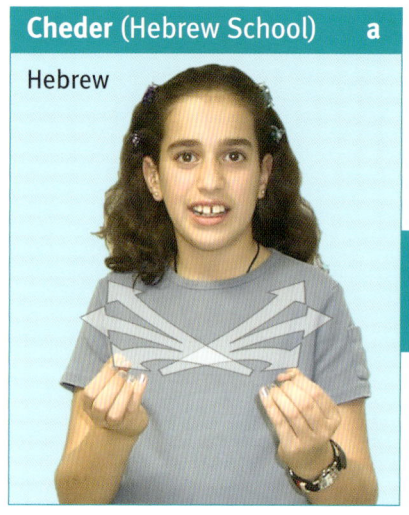

b

 **Fingertips together cross over and open**

c

School

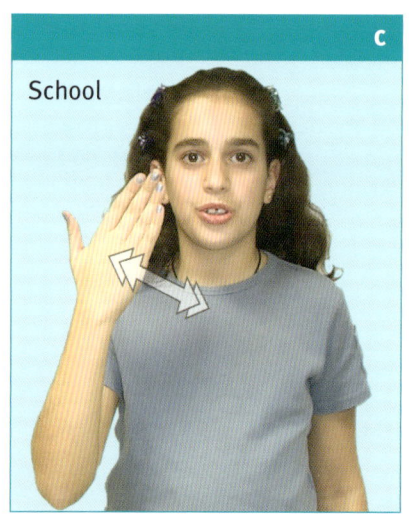

Religion school for Jewish children is also known as Cheder or Talmud Torah. It is usually held on the premises of a synagogue. Many Jewish children go there to learn about their religion in more depth than may be possible at school. Subjects include the study of Hebrew, Bible studies, Jewish laws and customs, and preparation for the Bar/Bat Mitzvah. Younger children are taught about Jewish customs, religious celebrations and history.

 **School**

 *Hey*-der

# Jewish Cycle of Life - Death

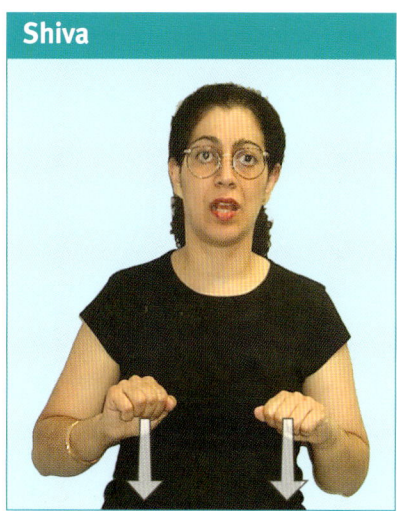

**Shiva**

 **Shi**-va

Shiva is the seven-day period of mourning that follows the death of a Jewish person.

Jewish tradition is that people are buried as soon as possible after death. Following the funeral, family and friends gather daily in the home of the deceased, or that of a near relative, to offer prayers, comfort and support to the mourners.  The official mourners – parents, spouse, children, brothers and sisters – sit on special low chairs (a traditional sign of mourning) to receive those who come to offer condolences.

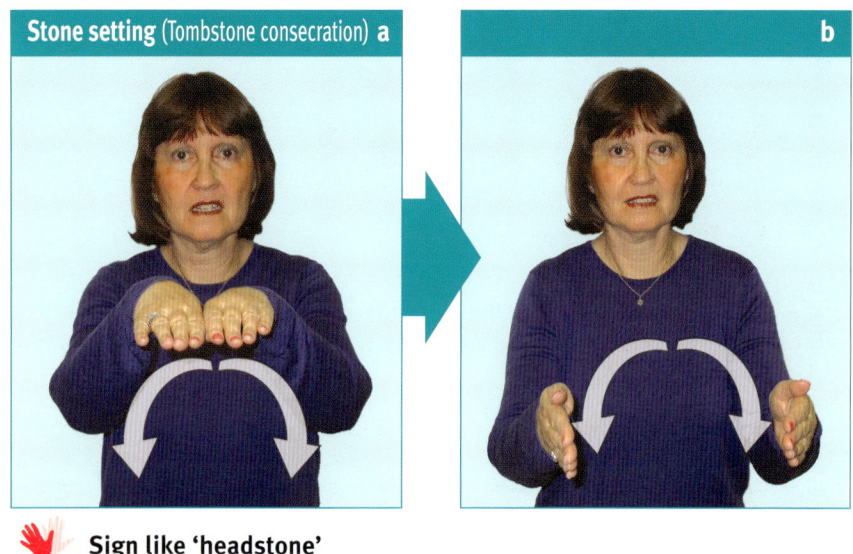

**Stone setting** (Tombstone consecration) **a**

**b**

Sign like 'headstone'

A memorial stone is placed over the grave of the deceased. It is customary to have a service to mark its dedication. The time between burial and dedication varies, in order to allow time for the earth to settle.

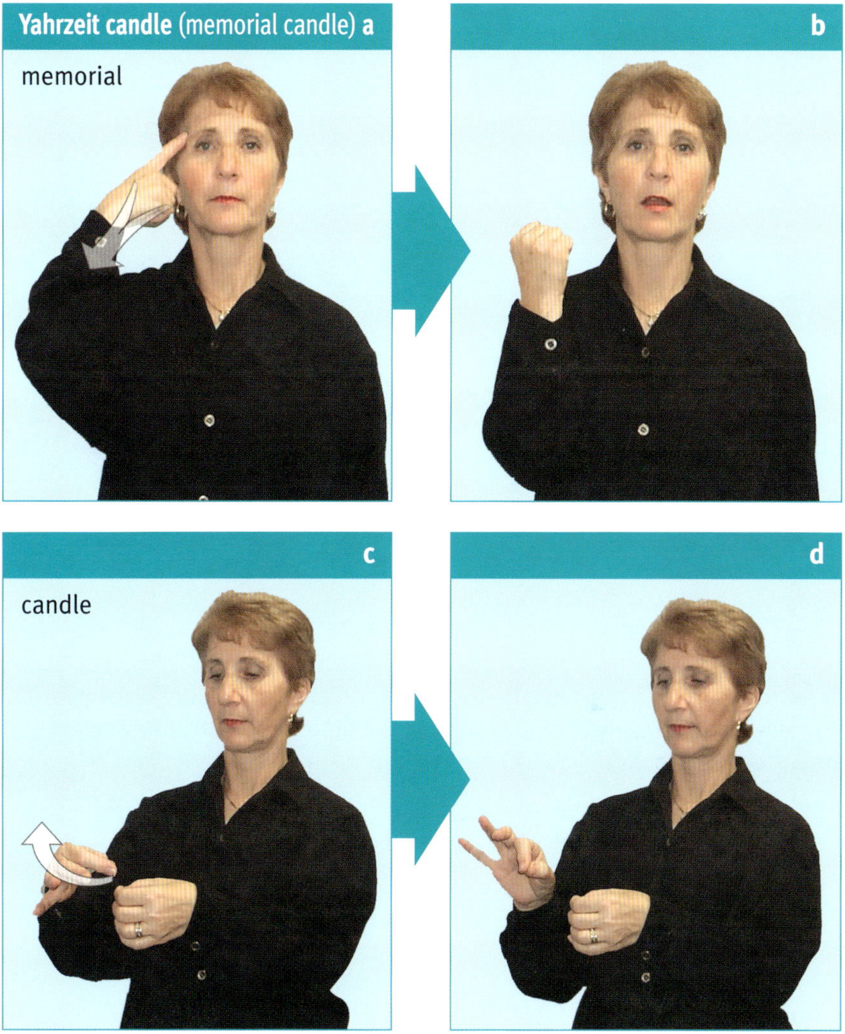

## Yahrzeit candle (memorial candle) a

memorial

b

c

candle

d

 **Sign like 'strike a match' outwards**

 Yart-zite (zite=like bite)

A Yahrzeit candle is a special memorial candle which burns for 24 hours. It is traditionally lit to mark the anniversary of the death of a close relative or loved one.

Yahrzeit candles are also lit on the Day of Atonement (Yom Kippur) and Holocaust Memorial Day (Yom Hashoah).

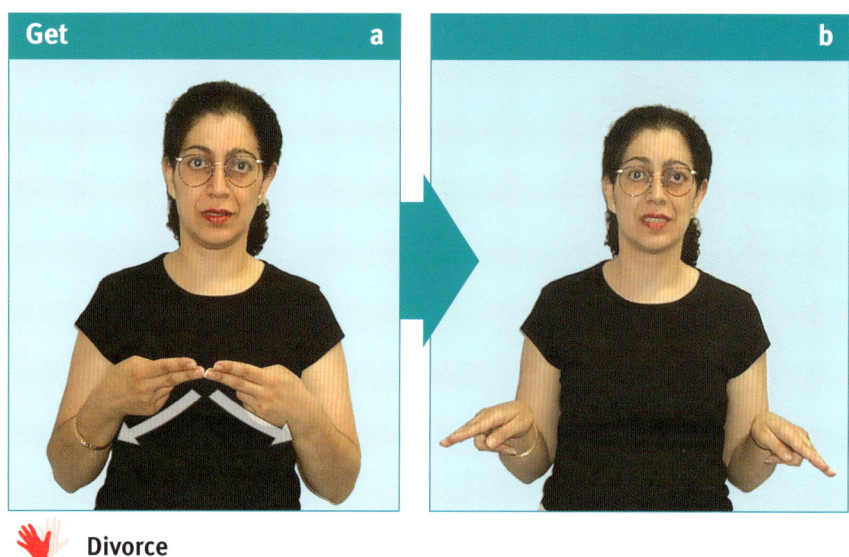

**Get** a

b

**Divorce**

A Jewish couple may divorce, if all efforts fail to revive a failing marriage. However, the woman will not be allowed to marry again unless she has been issued a document called a Get by the Rabbinical Court (Beth Din).

The reason for a Get is that as two people enter into a marriage of their own free will, it can only be ended by joint agreement.

# Jewish Cycle of Life - Marriage

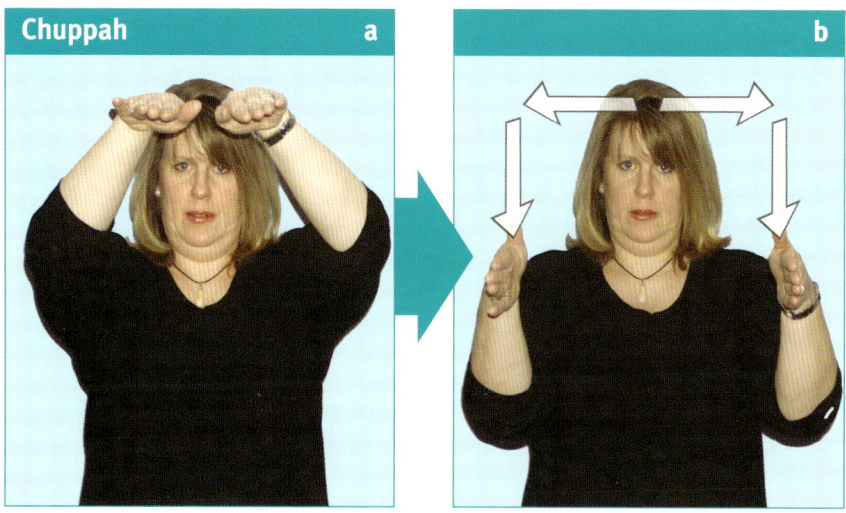

**Chuppah** a | b

*Hoo*-pa ("oo"=not oo as in "room" but oo as in "book")

The Chuppah is the canopy beneath which the marriage of a Jewish couple takes place.  It is open on four sides and supported by four poles, which sometimes stand alone or can be held by family members or friends.

The Chuppah represents the home which the couple will set up for themselves.

## Mikvah

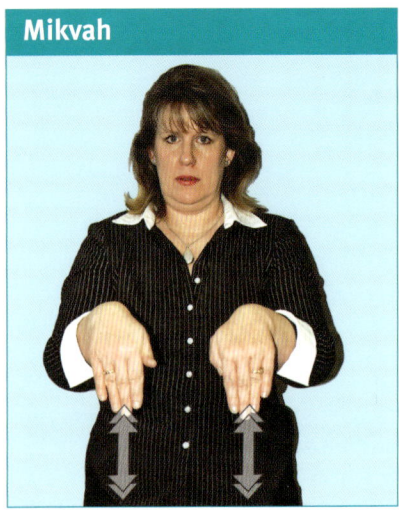

 **Mik**-va

The Mikvah is a pool of natural water used for purification purposes. The act of bathing in the Mikvah is an important religious duty in Judaism.

In traditional practice, a Jewish bride will visit the Mikvah on the night before her wedding and immerse herself in the water three times. She is then considered a purified woman. She will visit the Mikvah regularly throughout her married life.

Some religious Jewish men also immerse themselves in the Mikvah, some daily.

# Jewish Cycle of Life - Marriage

**Wedding**

 **Sign like 'putting a ring on a finger'**

Judaism requires marriage as the start of family life and a wedding is a cause for great celebration.

At the ceremony, the bride joins her waiting bridegroom under a canopy - the 'Chuppah'.

Seven blessings are recited and the marriage contract is read, in which the husband promises to care for and look after his wife. The contract is known as the Ketubah. The document is read and signed publicly and becomes the possession of the bride.

All present are reminded of the destruction of the Temple in Jerusalem. This act of remembrance is symbolised by the groom, who stamps on a glass and breaks it. This is a long-established custom.

# Signs in alphabetical order

# LUKE'S LOG

# LUKE'S LOG

K. D. Luke

JANUS PUBLISHING COMPANY
London, England

Janus Publishing Company Ltd,
105-107 Gloucester Place,
London W1U 6BY

www.januspublishing.co.uk

British Library Cataloguing-in-Publication Data
A catalogue record for this book is available
from the British Library

ISBN 1 85756 660 2

Cover Design: Mirela Zdjelaric

Printed and bound in Great Britain